TICKET TO THE OLYMPIC WINTER GAMES

MARTIN GITLIN

45th Parallel Press

Published in the United States of America by Cherry Lake Publishing Group
Ann Arbor, Michigan
www.cherrylakepublishing.com

Reading Adviser: Beth Walker Gambro, MS Ed., Reading Consultant, Yorkville, IL.

Photo Credits: © Xiao Yijiu/Xinhua/Alamy Live News, cover; © Toseef Yousaf/Shutterstock, inside cover, 13; © No-syrevy/Shutterstock, 2, 3, 6, 10, 16, 23, 32; kremlin.ru, CC BY 4.0 via Wikimedia Commons, 5; © Leonard Zhukovsky/Shutterstock, 7; Public Domain via Wikimedia Commons, 9; Vegar Samestad Hansen from Son, Norway, via Wikimedia Commons, 11; Public Domain, National Archives via Wikimedia Commons, 12; Henry Zbyszynski, CC BY 2.0 via Wikimedia Commons, 15; Public domain via Wikimedia Commons, 17; © Abaca Press / Alamy Stock Photo, 18; © Real Sports Photos/Shutterstock, 19; © Leonard Zhukovsky/Shutterstock, 21; © Asatur Yesayants/Shutterstock, 22; © Yakub88/Dreamstime.com, 24; © Smix Ryo/Shutterstock, 25, 29; © A. Emson/Shutterstock, 27; © Eugene Onischenko/Shutterstock, 28

45th Parallel Press is an imprint of Cherry Lake Publishing Group.

Library of Congress Cataloging-in-Publication Data

Names: Gitlin, Marty author
Title: Ticket to the Olympic Winter Games / by Martin Gitlin.
Description: Ann Arbor, Michigan : 45th Parallel Press, 2025. | Series: The big game | Audience: Grades 7-9 | Summary: "Who has won the Olympic Winter Games? How did they make it happen? Filled with high-interest text written with struggling readers in mind, this series includes fun facts, intriguing stories, and captivating play-by-plays from the world's most famous winter sports competition"-- Provided by publisher.
Identifiers: LCCN 2025009140 | ISBN 9781668963883 hardcover | ISBN 9781668965207 paperback | ISBN 9781668966815 ebook | ISBN 9781668968420 pdf
Subjects: LCSH: Winter Olympics--History--Juvenile literature
Classification: LCC GV841.5 .G57 2025 | DDC 796.9809--dcfull
LC record available at https://lccn.loc.gov/2025009140
Cherry Lake Publishing would like to acknowledge the work of The Partnership for 21st Century Skills. Please visit *www.p21.org* for more information.

Cherry Lake Publishing Group would like to acknowledge the work of the Partnership for 21st Century Learning, a Network of Battelle for Kids. Please visit Battelle for Kids online for more information.

Printed in the United States of America

Note from publisher: Websites change regularly, and their future contents are outside of our control. Supervise children when conducting any recommended online searches for extended learning opportunities.

Table of Contents

Introduction

Four years have passed. Athletes have been training. They've been testing their skills. They are the best of the best. They are ready.

Some ski down mountains. Others spin like tops on the ice. Hockey teams battle for the win.

Welcome to the Winter Olympic Games. They are held every 4 years. It is cold outside. But these games are on fire.

Athletes from all over the world compete. They want to be the best. They want to win medals for their countries. They want to be a **champion**. That is the best in their sport.

The waiting is over and the big game is about to begin. Opening ceremonies always kick off Olympic Games. Get ready, winter sports fans!

The Winter Olympic Games include 16 sports. The top athletes are often from cold-weather countries. Among them are Norway and Sweden.

Large countries with cold winters also do well. Included are Germany, Canada, Russia, and the United States. All send many athletes to the Games.

The top 3 athletes earn a medal. The third-place winner gets a bronze medal. Second place gets a silver medal. The first-place winner gets the gold medal. A gold medal means best in the world. How good do you have to be? Let's find out.

Let the big games begin!

Hanna Öberg of Sweden has won 2 olympic gold medals in the **biathlon**. This event pairs cross-country skiing with rifle sharpshooting.

History of the Game

The modern Olympics began in 1896. They were held in the summer. They were held every 4 years. They included figure skating and hockey.

Olympic officials had an idea in 1921. They wanted to add more winter sports. They wanted to start a Winter Games.

The first Winter Games were planned for 1924 in France. That country went to work. It built a skating rink. It built a ski jump. It built a **bobsled** track. A bobsled is a sled that slides down an icy track. Curling and hockey were the other two sports.

The Winter Olympics were about to begin. And they would get better and better during the next 100 years.

One of Great Britain's bobsled teams flies down the track at the 1924 Winter Olympic Games.

The Games have grown. The 1924 Winter Games had only 16 countries. They sent 258 athletes. The 2022 event had 91 countries. Nearly 3,000 athletes competed.

The Winter Games added 11 sports since 1924. It added downhill skiing in 1936. It added snowboarding in 1998.

Snowboarding is very popular. Athletes twist and turn on snow ramps and courses while standing on a board. Some of the other most popular sports are hockey, figure skating, and ski jumping.

The Summer and Winter Games were first held in the same host country. That changed quickly. It was too hard to host both. In 1928, the Winter Games took place in a different country than the Summer Games.

Olympic ceremonies grew. They added podiums. That was in 1932. Winners stood on the podiums. Gold medalists stood tallest. Silver medalists stood a step down. Bronze medalists stood on the lowest step.

Ski jumps can be up to 393.7 feet (120 meters) high. Athletes launch off of the jump. The one who lands the farthest from the jump is the winner!

A big change happened in the early 1990s. The Summer and Winter Games had been the same year before this. Both Games happened every 4 years. Many did not want to wait that long.

So the Games were split. There were Summer and Winter Olympics in 1992. Then there was another Winter Games in 1994. The Winter games took place every 4 years from there.

The first Olympic Winter Games following World War II (1939—1945) were in 1948. This is that year's U.S. Olympic Hockey Team.

It was January 6, 1994. The place was Cobo Arena. That is in Detroit, Michigan. Figure skater Nancy Kerrigan had finished practice. She was training for the U.S. Championships.

Kerrigan was removing her skates. A man with a metal baton approached. His name was Shane Stant. He slammed the baton on Kerrigan's knee. Then he ran away. Kerrigan cried out in pain.

Why did it happen? Many pointed to Tonya Harding. She was Kerrigan's skating rival. Her ex-husband hired Stant. Now Kerrigan couldn't compete. Harding won the U.S. Championships.

Kerrigan came back strong in February. That was at the Winter Olympics. Her knee had healed. Harding skated poorly. Kerrigan was great. She earned the silver medal.

Early Days, Big Moments

World events should not affect the Olympics. It is about **goodwill** between countries. Goodwill means good feelings. The event should focus on sports. But bad blood can steal the spotlight.

It did in 1980. That was during the Cold War (1947–1991). The Cold War was a standoff. It was between the United States and Soviet Union. The Soviet Union does not exist anymore. But it included Russia and 14 nearby countries.

Both the United States and Soviet Union had nuclear weapons. It was a dangerous time. Their hockey teams were set to clash. It was the Olympic **semifinal**. The winner would play for the gold medal.

Mike Ramsey of Team USA sets up the puck for a shot in the 1980 hockey Olympic semifinals.

The Soviets were strong. Their team was among the best in the world. The U.S. had only college players. At that time, the Olympics did not allow **professional athletes**. Those are paid athletes.

The Soviets scored first. That was no surprise. They kept shooting the puck to try to score goals. Jim Craig was the U.S. goaltender. Craig had to stop the puck from reaching the net.

Craig halted 36 shots. He allowed just 3 goals. Craig was just one hero in the game. Another was Mark Johnson. He scored in the third period. That tied it at 3–3.

Then it happened. U.S. player Mark Pavelich had the puck. He passed it to Mike Eruzione. Eruzione fired it toward the Soviet goal. It went past the goaltender. The Americans led, 4–3. It was the first time they were ahead.

The U.S. team held on for an amazing win. It was called "The Miracle on Ice."

Unexpected wins and surprising stars make the Winter Games exciting. Vonetta Flowers was a surprising star. She thrived in a summer sport in college. But she won gold in the Winter Olympics.

Mike Eruzione was the captain of the 1980 U.S. Olympic hockey team.

Flowers was a sprinter in college. She could run very fast. Flowers was also a star long jumper. She wanted to be a track star in the Summer Olympics. But injuries stopped her.

Flowers tried a new event. She worked on bobsledding. Flowers got very good.

She teamed with Jill Bakken. The duo won gold at the 2002 Winter Olympics. Flowers made Winter Games history. She was the first Black American to win gold at the Winter Games.

Sprinter Vonetta Flowers blossomed into a bobsledding star in the 2002 Games.

WAY BACK WHEN

Eric Heiden is a former American speedskater. He could skate about 35 miles (56.3 km) per hour!

Heiden is from Wisconsin. But he gained fame in Lake Placid. That is in New York. It hosted the 1980 Winter Olympics. Heiden dominated that year. He won all 5 speedskating events.

Each race is a different length. Most amazing was the 1,500-meter race. Heiden nearly fell halfway through. He dropped behind. It appeared he was doomed. But Heiden came back to win.

He finished with 5 gold medals. Heiden was the first speedskater to do that. He broke a world record in the 10,000-meter. That is the longest race.

Modern Moments

Shaun White had a wild nickname. He was "The Flying Tomato." One reason was his red hair. The other was that it seemed he really could fly.

White's sport was snowboarding. White won his first gold medal in 2006. It was in the **half-pipe** event. That is a curved snow ramp.

He did amazing tricks. He won gold again in 2010. He invented a trick called the "Tomahawk." That featured many twists in the air. White spun around nearly 4 times. Then he landed.

White struggled in 2014. He finished fourth in the half-pipe. But White returned in 2018. He again won Olympic gold. White retired after the 2022 Winter Games.

"The Flying Tomato" dominated snowboarding with his incredible tricks in 2006, 2010, and 2018.

Nathan Chen took home gold for himself and his team in 2022.

Another Winter Game standout is Nathan Chen. Nathan Chen is an American figure skater. Figure skaters dance on the ice. They leap and twist in the air. Chen was disappointed in 2018. He finished fifth in the Winter Olympics. Chen had to wait until 2022. Then he could try again.

Chen did better than try. He won his first gold medal. Chen won it for himself. But he also won it for his team. U.S. men rarely win in figure skating. It was their first gold in that sport since 2010.

Chen's total score of 332.6 topped the field. He amazed everyone. He did 2 **quadruple jumps**. Those are jumps with 4 twists in the air. It was no contest. Chen won the event easily.

Both White and Chen took home the gold in their sport. Ester Ledecká did one better. She took home the gold in 2 sports. Ledecká is from the Czech Republic in Europe. She is a snowboarder and a skier.

Ester Ledecká shows off her 2 Olympic gold medals and Snowboard World Cup trophy in 2018.

Ledecká competed in the 2018 Winter Games. She entered 2 events. The first was snowboarding. She won the gold medal. The second is alpine skiing. That is a downhill speed event. She won the gold medal in that, too. She made history.

But Ledecká was not done. She won snowboarding gold again in 2022. She had made history again. Many athletes from her country competed. But not one had won more Winter Games gold.

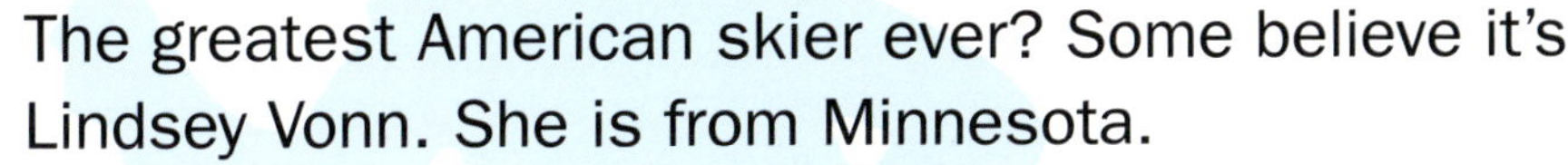

The greatest American skier ever? Some believe it's Lindsey Vonn. She is from Minnesota.

Vonn finished sixth overall in the 2002 Winter Olympics.

After that, she became famous before the 2006 Games. Vonn took a nasty fall during training. She worked hard to recover. Vonn won no medals that year. But it was amazing that she even competed.

Then she broke through. It was 2010. Vonn became an Olympic star. She won a gold medal. Vonn also took a bronze medal. That was for third place. She won another bronze in the 2018 Games.

LEGEND OF THE SPORT

Rising Stars

Keep an eye on these rising stars. They might soon become legends!

Camilla Vanni

Teenagers often compete in the Games. Anyone 13 or older can bc on an American team. But some sports are too hard for young teens.

One is downhill skiing. Camilla Vanni knows that. She is from Italy. Vanni was 15 in 2022. She was not ready for the Winter Olympics. But her future was bright.

She proved it in the Youth Olympic Games. That is held every 4 years. It is for teenage athletes. Vanni won an alpine skiing event. She finished in under 54 seconds. Nobody else did that.

Whoever completes the alpine ski course fastest wins! This takes a lot of skill.

Daxon Rudolph

Hockey players work hard to score goals. They want to shoot the puck into a net. Or they want an **assist**. That is a pass that leads to a goal.

Top players average one goal or assist per game. Canadian Daxon Rudolph did better than that. Rudolph played youth hockey. He played 82 games. He scored 41 goals. He added 92 assists. That was incredible.

The Prince Albert Raiders junior hockey team came calling. They are in the Western Hockey League. Rudolph joined the Raiders. He hopes to be on Canada's Olympic team someday. Turning 17 in 2025, he has years to make that dream happen.

Canada is known for its hockey players. Daxon Rudolph is sure to shine.

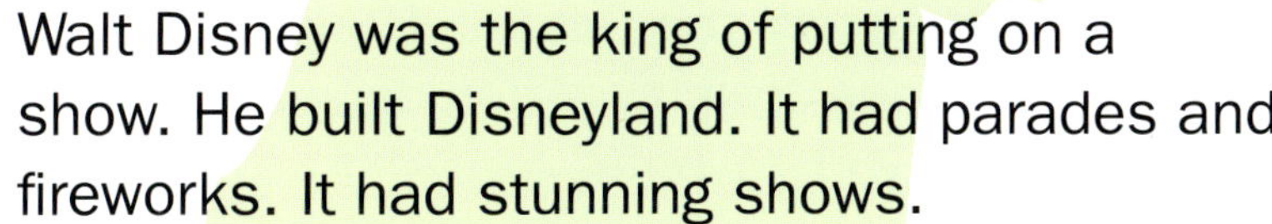

Walt Disney was the king of putting on a show. He built Disneyland. It had parades and fireworks. It had stunning shows.

Disney brought his skills to the 1960 Winter Games. He organized the opening event. He changed the ceremony forever. He made it big. He made it stunning.

The crowd heard high school bands play. Thousands of balloons were released. They soared into the air. Fireworks blasted. They showed many colors and designs.

About 2,000 homing pigeons were released. They fluttered away. Flags of nations were dropped from the sky. They were brought in by parachute. Walt Disney really knew how to put on a show!

! A BIT OF TRIVIA

Activity

Study the Winter Games. Read books and go online with an adult. Learn about the history of the Games. Find out more about the greatest Winter Games athletes. Then decide your favorite sport. Write about why it's your favorite.

Take the next step. Get your friends and classmates involved. Ask them to learn more about the event. Then they can decide their favorite sport. They can choose their favorite athletes.

You could watch the next Winter Games together. Plan a watch party for your favorite events. You can keep track of wins. You can cheer for your favorite athletes!

Learn More

BOOKS

Buckley, James Jr. *Miracle on Ice! The U.S. Hockey Team in the 1980 Winter Olympics.* Minneapolis, MN: Bearport Publishing, 2024.

Gitlin, Martin. *Miracle on Ice.* Ann Arbor, MI: Cherry Lake Publishing, 2024.

Herman, Gail. *What Are the Winter Olympics?* New York, NY: Penguin Workshop, 2021.

WEBSITES

Search these online sources with an adult.

National Geographic Kids | 10 WINTER OLYMPICS FACTS!

Twinkl | Winter Olympics for Kids! video | Winter Olympics 2022

Glossary

animation (aa-nuh-MAY-shuhn) cartoon movies and TV shows

assist (uh-SIST) hockey pass that leads to a goal

biathlon (by-ATH-luhn) a competition that pairs cross-country skiing with rifle sharpshooting

bobsled (BAHB-sled) sled that slides fast down an icy track

champion (CHAM-pee-uhn) winner in a league or sport

goodwill (gud-WIL) good feelings between people or countries

half-pipe (HAF-piyp) curved, high-sided snow ramp

professional athletes (pruh-FESH-nuhl ATH-leets) athletes who are paid to play

quadruple jumps (kwah-DROO-puhl JUMPS) figure skating jumps with 4 twists in the air

semifinal (seh-mee-FIYE-nuhl) game in which the winner advances to play for a gold medal or championship

Index

About the Author

Martin Gitlin is an educational book author based in Connecticut. He won more than 45 awards as a newspaper sportswriter from 1991 to 2002. Included was a first-place award from the Associated Press for his coverage of the 1995 World Series. He has had more than 200 books published since 2006. Most of them were written for students.